Backstage at a
PLAY

Kimberly M. Miller

HIGH
interest
books

Children's Press®
A Division of Scholastic Inc.
New York / Toronto / London / Auckland / Sydney
Mexico City / New Delhi / Hong Kong
Danbury, Connecticut

Book Design: Daniel Hosek and Chris Logan
Contributing Editor: Matthew Pitt
Photo Credits: Cover, pp. 7, 12, 17 © Robbie Jack/Corbis; p. 4 © Steve
Raymer/Corbis, pp. 8, 21, 28 © Bettmann/Corbis; p. 11 © Adam Woolfitt;
p. 15, 18 © William E. Sauro/New York Times Co./Getty Images; pp. 22, 30
© James A. Sugar/Corbis; p. 25 © Stan Sherer; pp. 26, 35 © Tom Stewart/
Corbis; p. 32 © Kelly-Mooney Photography/Corbis; p. 36 © Mitchell
Gerber/Corbis; p. 39 © Jacques M. Chenet/Corbis; p. 41 © Nubar
Alexanian/Corbis

Library of Congress Cataloging-in-Publication Data

Miller, Kimberly M.
    Backstage at a play / Kimberly M. Miller.
    p. cm. — (Backstage pass)
    Includes bibliographical references and index.
    Summary: Provides a behind the scenes look at plays.
    ISBN 0-516-24327-6 (lib. bdg.) — ISBN 0-516-24389-6 (pbk.)
    1. Theater—Juvenile literature. 2. Theater—Production and
direction—Juvenile literature. I. Title. II. Series.

PN2037 .M49 2003
792—dc21

                                          2002010893

CONTENTS

Butterflies may develop in the stomachs of a cast and crew before opening night. Once the curtain rises, however, they must set their anxieties aside.

Introduction

In the darkness of the theater, you hold your breath. You can just make out the footsteps of your fellow actors stepping lightly beside you. Suddenly, someone whispers in your ear, "Five minutes, please. You're on in five."

You take a deep breath—you're about to perform in front of an audience. As soon as you walk onstage, you'll take on a different identity. Each time you act in a play, you portray an entirely different person. In one role, you played the president of the United States. In another, you played a character that came from a faraway nation and spoke with a foreign accent. For each role, you had to change your style of walking, speaking, and moving to make the transformation complete.

Of course, the entire theater has gone through a similar transformation. Just six weeks ago, this stage was bare. No set had been built for the actors to walk upon. There were no brilliant, colorful lights to stand beneath. Costume designers hadn't even started sewing your wardrobe.

Taking a play from page to stage involves huge amounts of planning. Many different talents are on display. Actors play the most visible part of a theater production, but not the only one. Making a script come alive requires dedicated writers, designers, artists, and set builders. Everyone works hard to put on a great performance—one that will provide the cast, crew, and audience with enough surprises and magic to last a lifetime.

You clear your throat. There's no more time to think. The curtain is rising!

One of the jobs of a gifted theater actor is to make each show feel unique. That's a tricky task—especially if you're in a smash hit like *Rent*, which may have hundreds of shows during its run.

The Globe playhouse quickly became England's hottest
ticket once it was built in 1599.

CHAPTER ONE

On With the Show

The art of theater has been developing for centuries. It began as a way to share stories, information, and feelings with large groups of people. In theater, actors use eloquent dialogue, expressive movements, and music to recount sad tales, love stories, comedies, and even dramatic battles.

MUCH ADO ABOUT SOMETHING

In sixteenth-century England, theater became very popular. Citizens were delighted when traveling troupes, or groups of performers, visited their towns to put on plays. One inspired theatergoer from that time was William Shakespeare. Shakespeare became the world's most famous playwright, or writer of plays. His plays were first performed at the Globe. The Globe was a permanent playhouse, or theater, located in London.

The Globe had a raked stage. A raked stage is higher at the back and lower at the front.

This design helped provide all audience members with a complete view of the onstage action.

During Shakespeare's time, there were no electric lights or microphones. Performers had to find creative ways to be seen and heard. Actors learned to project their voices. They trained to speak loudly, yet clearly. This helped even those audience members seated far away to understand the actors' lines.

Not only was the Globe's stage raked, but it also extended into the audience. This gave customers a better view of the actors. The Globe's

ALL THE WORLD'S A STAGE

While theater is a global art form, its styles change from culture to culture. In parts of Africa, people have acted out the same stories for generations. These stories teach people what their society expects of them. Italy's Renaissance-era commedia dell'arte plays are often bizarre or gross. Yet they're always wildly funny. Japan has created many dramatic theatrical forms. Several of them use music and dance in exciting, innovative ways. Noh theater focuses on movement and broad gestures. Performers often wear expressive masks carved out of cedar. Another form, Kabuki, was developed in the 1600s. Although a woman created Kabuki, women are not allowed to act in these plays. Instead, men called *onnagata* play the female roles.

roof was open, allowing daylight to stream into the theater. Plays were always performed during daylight hours. This schedule didn't please shop owners—their employees often skipped work to catch the latest shows!

ROYAL TREATMENT

Kings and queens who attended plays sat in special balconies. Most audience members, however, simply paid a penny to stand in the yards, or standing room section, around the stage. These audience

Shakespeare's plays truly had his fans standing in the aisle. Any audience member who couldn't afford a balcony seat was forced to stand through the entire show.

Shakespeare was famous for writing strong-willed, intelligent female characters. Ironically, women of the time were prevented from giving life to the very roles written for them. Here, a man plays the role of Cleopatra.

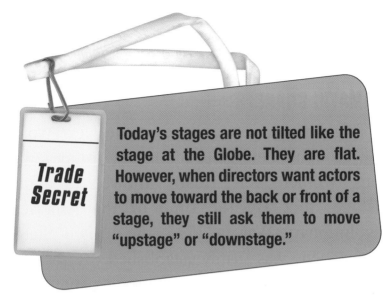

Trade Secret

Today's stages are not tilted like the stage at the Globe. They are flat. However, when directors want actors to move toward the back or front of a stage, they still ask them to move "upstage" or "downstage."

members were called groundlings. The groundlings were about eye level to the stage. All of the action was in their face—literally! Fake blood spilled from actors who were wounded or killed in onstage battles. Magical witches and fairies turned people into animals. Passionate love scenes were also a big part of the plays. However, showing the love scenes was a challenge because all the actors were men. At the time, society considered it immoral for women to appear onstage.

How were the Globe's plays different from traveling shows? Actors at the Globe no longer improvised, or made up lines as they performed. Instead, playwrights such as Shakespeare were paid to write the actors' dialogue.

DRAMATIC CHANGES

As English colonists arrived in the New World, they brought their beloved theater troupes with them. Women were finally allowed to appear onstage, too. By the time of the American Revolutionary War in 1775, the United States' theater scene was firmly established.

New York City quickly claimed its spot as the young nation's top theater city. The playhouses built there in the nineteenth and twentieth centuries were very different from those of Shakespeare's time. Stages no longer stretched out into the audience. Flat proscenium stages took their place. Proscenium stages have arches that frame the stage, separating the actors from the spectators. Proscenium stages also provide hidden spaces, called wings, on either side of the stage. Actors wait in the wings before appearing onstage. There, actors can also change costumes and prepare without being seen by the audience. This strengthens the illusion of the play.

Thanks to the invention of the electric light in the late 1800s, shows could now be performed at night.

For many Americans, theater is a beloved form of expression. New York City's oldest playhouse, the Lyceum Theater, was named a national landmark in 1978.

Electric theater lights were attached to metal bars. Electricians attached several metal bars together to make up a grid. The grid was lifted high above the stage. Electricians lowered the grid at the right moment during the play to help create dazzling lighting effects. For instance, a scene that took place during a storm might feature lights that flashed on and off to resemble lightning.

PLAY ON!

During the Great Depression of the 1930s, the U.S. government built new theaters all over the country. The government recognized the importance of lifting the nation's spirits during this troubled time. It created the Federal Theatre Project, which gave jobs to unemployed actors, electricians, and carpenters. It also provided struggling Americans with inexpensive, inspiring entertainment. Many of these theaters, such as those in Cleveland, Ohio, and San Diego, California, remain open today.

The theater delights many fans by experimenting and leaping away from reality. In the Argentinean hit, *De La Guarda*, performers launch across the stage using acrobatics and bungee cords. They're even known to lift some of their audience members with them!

From Eugene O'Neill and Arthur Miller to Wendy Wasserstein, America has produced dozens of great playwrights. Perhaps none loom larger, though, than Thomas "Tennessee" Williams (pictured).

CHAPTER TWO

Major Players

THE MAKING OF A PLAY

Before a play can be performed onstage, it must grab the attention of one very important person: the producer. Producers choose the scripts that will be performed onstage. They hire the talented, dedicated people who bring the play to life. They also find people and businesses willing to invest money in the show. Another major player in the process of creating a play is the director. This chapter follows a new production of Tennessee Williams's famous play, *A Streetcar Named Desire*. We'll trace each step of the production through the eyes of the play's director, Ailene Mitchell.

AILENE'S STORY

"When a few big-name producers decided to bring a Tennessee Williams play back to Broadway, I'm the first one they called. After all, my updates of theater classics from Shakespeare to Oscar Wilde have delighted crowds for years.

"You might have seen *A Streetcar Named Desire* before. The clothes, music, and set are all obviously from another time. My job is to create a fresh, modern vision for the play. I'll study the script constantly, looking for its spine, or major themes. I'll audition and hire a cast. At rehearsals, I must create an atmosphere of trust and freedom with my actors. I'll search for ways to make the play exciting and meaningful to modern audiences.

"Tennessee Williams set *Streetcar* in a section of New Orleans, Louisiana, called the French Quarter. In the 1940s, it was a rough part of town. These days, though, the French Quarter is a tourist spot. So I'm changing the setting of my *Streetcar* to Dallas, Texas. The original play opens with Blanche coming to visit her younger sister, Stella, in New Orleans. Blanche has to tell Stella she's lost the family's cotton plantation in the Old South. In our version, it's the family's cattle ranch in West Texas that she loses. Blanche travels to Dallas to give her sister the bad news."

SET TO BEGIN

Professional directors like Ailene meet with their designers many times before rehearsals begin. At the meetings, Ailene and her designers share ideas. They bounce concerns and questions off one another. This way, the crew can quickly identify problems and create inspiring solutions.

Like other great plays, *A Streetcar Named Desire* showcases characters with complex personalities. Some are delicate yet deceptive, while others are loyal but cruel. Williams's wonderful play (shown here) won the Pulitzer Prize in 1948.

This process of working together is called collaboration—and it's the lifeblood of theater.

"Our set designer, Cedric, starts off our first meeting. He unveils a miniature model of the Dallas set. It shows that Stella, her husband Stanley, and her sister Blanche will live in a cramped apartment. Old industrial buildings, such as factories,

A play such as Samuel Beckett's *Endgame* presents a challenge to set designers. Their designs must reflect the absurdity of Beckett's script. On the other hand, the cast must be able to easily walk around the set.

surround the apartment. This means that people are working in the neighborhood twenty-four hours a day. It's always crowded and always loud.

"Whenever the play's action occurs outside, we'll roll a set piece in front of the main set. This set piece will include the outside of Stanley and Stella's apartment building. However, it'll just be a façade, or the building's front. The façade will have smashed windowpanes and peeled paint. These touches will remind viewers that this is a poor part of town. Each time we roll in the façade, background characters who have jobs in the neighborhood, such as fortunetellers and paperboys, will drift by.

"Cedric has done a great job capturing a dark, edgy feel. His set design reminds me of an important point that I tell the designers to keep in mind. Because Blanche and Stella come from a wealthy family, Blanche must be shocked at her sister's dumpy surroundings. She must seem like a fish out of water in this unfamiliar environment.

"My comment inspires Wayne, our sound designer. He decides to add a few sound effects of factory equipment during the play's tense scenes.

In certain lines of the script, Blanche complains that her nerves are in knots. When those lines occur, Wayne will add amplified sounds of workers' boots stomping and car engines rattling."

LET THERE BE LIGHT

"Aimee and Dave, our lighting design team, have some brilliant ideas of how to light Blanche. Blanche is in her mid-forties. She is always trying to hide her age. She goes out of her way to avoid being seen clearly. Aimee and Dave created a special lighting style just for her character. The rooms in the set will have bright spots that look like they're lit by just one bulb. Blanche will lurk around the corners.

"As the play progresses, Aimee and Dave will gradually dim the amount of light, creating dark shadows around Blanche. They also plan to cast Blanche in red light whenever she's upset or nervous. To do this, they'll place colored transparencies, called gels, over the light fixtures hanging from the grid.

"Our costume designer, Sheila, believes that most of the cast should dress casually. This will show that the characters don't have much cash to spend on high fashion. Sheila will have the actors wear jeans. Guys will wear T-shirts. Women can wear work shirts or house dresses. Sheila's going to wash and scrub the costumes several times to give them a faded, worn look. She'll add oil stains to the guys' T-shirts to show they've been working all day.

Wild farces such as *The Wall of Water*, by Sherry Kramer, often require complicated technical aspects. This production even features a raked stage. In the scene pictured here, a special lighting cue spotlights a character as he ascends to the heavens.

"Blanche is a different story. She's a little out of touch, so she overdresses for every occasion. Since she's lost all her money, however, she can't buy anything new. Her wardrobe reflects this. Sheila's going to dress Blanche in old prom dresses. She checks with Aimee and Dave about coordinating

Actors have to carry their scripts through early rehearsals. Once they've memorized the dialogue, they are considered "off book."

color schemes. This way, the lighting won't wash out the color of the dresses."

MANAGED CARE

Hundreds of problems can disrupt or threaten a production. A good stage manager can help make the production a smooth experience. Once Ailene heard her favorite stage manager, Mark Thomas, was joining the crew, her confidence soared.

"Mark will be my right-hand man as the show develops. On a copy of the script, he'll write detailed notes describing the blocking. Blocking refers to the movements each actor makes during the course of the play. He'll also keep track of every single prop. Props are accessories, such as the cigarette lighter, drinking glasses, and plates used by the play's characters.

"Mark will make sure my cast and crew always know when they're needed at the theater. He'll keep track of all lighting and sound cues, or technical signals. He'll make notes of each actor's entrances and exits onstage and offstage. During rehearsals, he'll jot down every suggestion I give my cast."

Andrew Lloyd Webber's *Cats* was praised by its fans for the show's great music and acting. Many critics, however, didn't find the show to be "the cat's meow."

CHAPTER THREE

Production in Progress

Three days before opening night, Ailene, her cast, and her technical crew meet for a special kind of rehearsal called a cue tech. At a cue tech, actors deliver lines without inflection. Inflection is changing the tone or pitch of your voice when you speak. It's what gives your words the emotions you feel.

The crew carefully watches the cast run through their blocking. This way, the designers will know where the actors are on the set, what they're saying, and when it's time for a technical cue. During one scene, Stanley throws a bottle into a window. The window is bare. Wayne, however, plans to cue a sound effect of breaking glass. To time this cue perfectly, Wayne needs to know which line Stanley says just before he throws the bottle.

A few weeks before the cue tech, the designers attended an early rehearsal. They created light and sound cues at several places throughout the script.

With an hour to go before curtain, the dressing room bursts with activity and excitement.

Aimee and Dave drew a diagram of where to hang the lights. Later, electricians flew, or lowered, the grid down to ground level. They hung the lights to match the designers' diagram.

Now, at the cue tech, the designers find out if their bright ideas will work. When the actors reach a cue, Ailene asks them to repeat the line. The light and soundboard operators test the cue out. Sometimes, a cue looks and sounds great right away. Other times, designers discover that the spotlight or burst of music they imagined would be perfect for the play is actually awkward. If this occurs, the designers must rethink the cue. An electrician might have to adjust a light or change a gel. A cue tech often takes twice as long as a normal rehearsal.

OPENING NIGHT

7:00 P.M. Actors arrive at the theater and sign a board before heading to their dressing rooms. Mark will be able to check this board later, to make certain the entire cast has arrived. Makeup artists begin to apply stage makeup to each cast member.

7:30 P.M. Mark announces that there are 30 minutes remaining until curtain, the moment the show begins. "Costumes, everyone!" he yells. The cast rushes to wardrobe, where Sheila's assistants help them into their clothes.

7:50 P.M. "Places," Mark shouts. "Everyone break a leg!" That's not really what he means, though. It's just an expression theater people use to wish each other a good performance. A traditional theater belief is that wishing bad luck on an actor will cause good luck to occur.

8:00 P.M. Actors are in their places, ready for the curtain to rise. Blanche is onstage, a suitcase in her hand.

The play begins with her arriving in Dallas, viewing this strange, unfamiliar town. Stella and Stanley are waiting in the wings. The theater, often called the house, is packed. The atmosphere backstage crackles with excitement as Mark asks the house: "Please take your seats. The performance is about to begin." Stagehands raise the curtain on Blanche.

When a seam splits during a scene, talented costume designers may only have moments to stitch it back together.

In her first scene with Stanley, Blanche forgets some of her blocking. She walks too close to Stanley. When he tries to get out of her way, he steps on her dress and tears it. The actor playing Stanley whispers to Blanche that the tear is not serious. The actors continue performing as if nothing's wrong.

8:25 P.M. Scene 1 ends. The actors exit stage left and stage right. Wardrobe knows about the torn dress. A seamstress is waiting for Blanche in the wings with a needle and thread. The seamstress has to sew fast— Blanche must be back onstage in 5 minutes! The repairs are finished with seconds to spare.

AS LUCK WOULD HAVE IT

Theater crews and performers tend to be a superstitious bunch. Some believe it's bad luck to whistle backstage. Many crews leave a small light onstage 24 hours a day. They believe this beacon, called a ghost light, wards off bad luck. There's a lot of lore surrounding Shakespeare's thirty-ninth script, *Macbeth*, which is set in Scotland. It's believed that more accidents and injuries occur during productions of *Macbeth* than any other play. Many performers refuse to even say *Macbeth* by name. They only dare call it "the Scottish play."

8:45 P.M. Scene 3 is about to begin. Since Blanche's dress was fixed, everything has gone well. The cues for scene 2 worked perfectly. None of the cast has dropped, or forgotten, a line. In scene 3, Stella and Blanche are returning from a night out. Stanley and his friends are at the apartment. They're supposed to be playing poker.

When the lights go up, Mark realizes there's no deck of cards on the poker table! All the lines are about a card game. While Mark looks for the cards backstage, the actors improvise to fill time. They shuffle things around on the table and pretend to talk to each other in low voices. When one cast member sees Mark holding the deck offstage, he thinks quickly. "That deck is missing an ace!" he says to the others. "I'm getting a new pack." When he walks back onstage with the deck of cards he takes from Mark, everyone takes a deep breath. They've pulled it off, and the show will go on!

9:00 P.M. The actors file off the stage at intermission. For 15 minutes, they have a chance to relax. Most of the actors change costumes. They discuss the audience's reactions to their performance. The actress who plays Stella also tells Stanley she's going to say one of her lines a bit differently than she has in rehearsals. Experimenting with the play keeps things fresh. At Mark's signal, the cast takes the stage for the final act. After the play concludes, the cast will bow and receive curtain calls from their delighted audience.

It's critical for a play's cast to get along and have fun. The trust they build during rehearsals often carries over to opening night.

Are *you* ready for your curtain call? These talented actors followed their dreams down the yellow-brick road—and so can you!

CHAPTER FOUR

Is Theater in Your *Blood?*

What kind of person becomes an actor? A director? A member of the technical crew? Each role is crucial to the success of theater. No matter what your job, creativity is a must. You must be able to generate a constant stream of unique ideas. Can you think fast on your feet? You may need to— most plays are rehearsed, designed, and produced in only a few weeks.

Being able to collaborate with others is also a must. It's easy to get upset when things aren't working well. If you get a reputation in theater circles for being difficult to work with, it could ruin your career.

CLASS ACT

Your school might have a theater program and drama teachers. Get involved. Enroll in drama classes. Drama classes are a great way to pick up acting techniques. Drama teachers often have students perform scenes for their classmates. Your fellow students become your first audience! If you give a command performance, you may catch your drama coach's eye. He or she may, in turn, have their eye on you for the lead in the next school play or musical.

What if you crave the spotlight, but aren't enrolled in a drama class? No problem—you can still audition for plays. Most schools hold open auditions, where anyone can try out. Audition notices are often posted on school bulletin boards. Find out ahead of time how the audition will work. Will the drama teacher provide scenes from the play for the actors to read? Will you be expected to memorize lines from another play? Some drama teachers may want to test your range. They might ask you to memorize one comedic and one dramatic monologue.

If you land a role, don't worry if it's small. Instead, spend every moment you're not onstage listening to, and learning from, more experienced actors. In your spare time, perform scenes from other plays with your friends. All you need is your imagination.

GET TECHNICAL

Of course, your interests may lie behind the scenes. If so, you'll need some technical training. Learn how to run the light or soundboards. Ask if you can be a production's stage manager. This job will give you great insight into every other job in a production. Gain enough experience, and you may be

Some theater artists crave the spotlight—others, however, are much more concerned with operating and aiming the spotlight.

allowed to direct a one-act or full-length play of your own. Even if you're positive you're a born performer, it's good to try your hand at theater's technical side. It will help you understand how different elements work together to form one show.

TAKE YOUR ACT ON THE ROAD

Volunteer at your town's community theater. Ushers often get to see the shows for free. Ask if the set builders have carpentry or painting to do. Maybe the costumers need a hand with some last-minute sewing. If you prove that you're quick thinking and reliable, you may be asked back to help out again.

Many people working in the theater don't have regular nine-to-five jobs. Working on plays often means working late. Performers spend long hours memorizing their lines and attending rehearsals. Lighting designers often spend all day running cue tech. Once finished, it takes hours longer to test the lighting board and perfect the cues. Theater people are always working hard, but it is a labor of love. Whether you wind up onstage or backstage, have fun, take some risks—and break a leg!

Theater casts and crews work night after night learning lines and perfecting cues. When the curtain closes, they know they've earned their bows, bravos, and standing ovations.

blocking the movements actors make while onstage

commedia del'arte an Italian form of comedy

cue a signal that alerts an actor or crewmember
  to do something

cue tech a rehearsal during which a play's technical
  aspects are practiced

downstage the area of the stage closest to the
  audience; the lower part of a raked stage

façade a false front of a building used on stage sets

gels colored transparent sheets that add color to
  electric lights

grid a series of metal bars upon which a play's
  electric lights are hung

house the audience that has come to view
  a performance

Kabuki a type of Japanese drama usually performed
  by men in elaborate costumes

Noh a form of Japanese theater in which performers wear expressive masks

playwright someone who writes plays

project to make one's voice carry very far

prop an item an actor needs to carry or use onstage

proscenium stage a stage on which most of the action takes place behind an archway separating the actor from the audience

raked stage a sloped stage used to give the audience members farthest from the stage a better view

spine a play's major theme or message

upstage the area of the stage farthest from the audience; the highest part of a raked stage

wings
  wh

yards
  gro

Books

Greenspon, Jaq. *Acting*. New York: McGraw Hill, 1996.

Huberman, Caryn, and Joanne S. Wetzel. *Onstage/Backstage*. Minneapolis, MN; Lerner Publishing Group, 1987.

Langley, Andrew. *Shakespeare's Theatre*. New York: Oxford University Press, 1999.

Sotnak, Lewann. *Director: Film, TV, Radio, and Stage*. Mankato, MN: Capstone Press, 2000.

Stevens, Chambers. *Magnificent Monologues for Kids (Hollywood 101)*. South Pasadena, CA: Sandcastle Publishing, 1999.

Williams, Tennessee. *A Streetcar Named Desire*. New York: Signet, 1951.

Organizations

Actors Equity Association
165 West 46th Street
New York, NY 10036
(212) 869-8530

**The International Association of Theater for
Children and Young People (ASSITEJ/USA)**
724 Second Avenue South
Nashville, TN 37210
(615) 254-5719
www.assitej-usa.org
The U.S. center of the ASSITEJ is dedicated to
promoting and providing theater for young people
and their families.

Web Sites

Tada! Youth Theater

www.tadatheater.com

You can find exciting internships, acting classes, and audition opportunities on this Web site. The site also introduces playful theater games you can try with friends.

All Theatre Arts

www.alltheatrearts.com

This site features several online articles that give you in-depth information about the roles of theater directors, producers, and performers.

Creative Drama & Theatre for Youth Webring

www.amergin.net/cdytmain.html

Provides Web surfers with links to hundreds of other sites relating to the dramatic arts.

INDEX

About the Author

Kimberly M. Miller has appeared in many theatrical productions staged in Texas, in which she wore a variety of absurd costumes. Since moving to New York City, she has retired from the stage. She is still drawn to the bright lights, however, and attends Broadway plays whenever she gets the chance.